Cambridgeshire and Huntingdonshire's Lost Railways
Neil Burgess

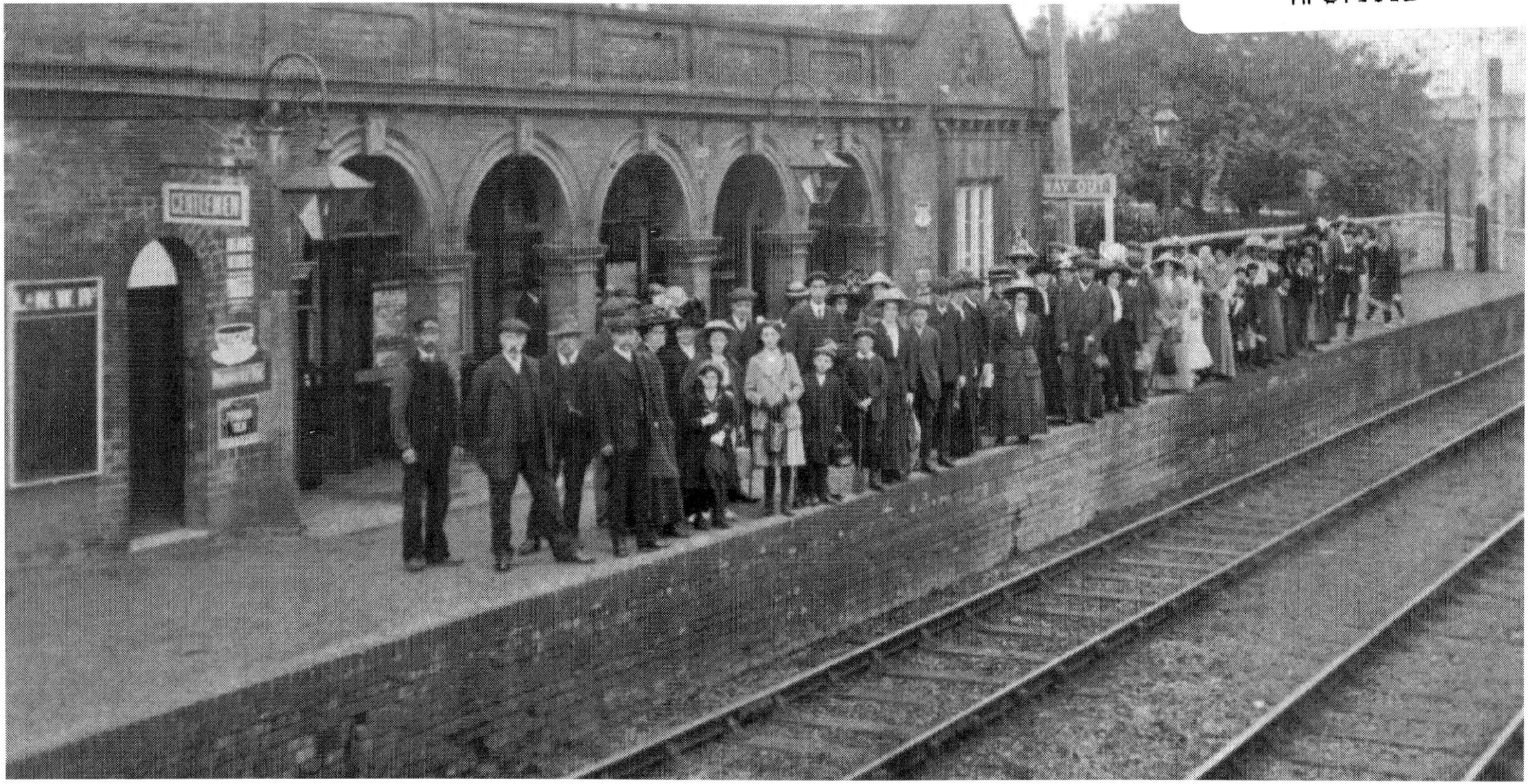

A crowd waits for a train at Chatteris Station, on the St Ives to March line, at the start of their journey to Yarmouth, 8 August 1912. They are travelling for the August Bank Holiday which was held at the beginning of the month until 1965.

Text © Neil Burgess, 2023
First published in the United Kingdom, 2023,
by Stenlake Publishing Ltd.
www.stenlake.co.uk
ISBN 978-1-84033-952-9

The publishers regret that they cannot supply
copies of any pictures featured in this book.

Printed by
P2D Books, 1 Newlands Rd, Westoning, Bedford MK45 5LD

Picture Credits

The publishers would like to thank John Alsop for the front, back and inside front cover photographs, and those on pages 1, 2, 4, 5, 9, 10, 12-16, 18-22, 24-31, 33, 35-37, 40-42 and 44-47.

Closure Dates

This book lists dates when stations and lines were closed to regular scheduled passenger traffic. Readers need to recognise that sources vary in deciding closure dates, some giving the last day on which regular services operated, others the first day when closure was effected and no passenger traffic operated. Especially on lines with no regular Sunday service, this might yield a discrepancy of two days, depending on the method used.

In some cases, particularly before the mid-1960s, stations along closed lines may have been left substantially intact and periodically excursion trains called to pick up or set down passengers. Where sources indicate that this happened it may be noted in the text, but it does not affect the official closure date.

Long Stanton looking to the level crossing, *c.* 1900. The station buildings are on the left.

Introduction

Cambridgeshire and Huntingdonshire form the north-western edge of East Anglia, both of them part of the historic fenland region. Before the fens were drained, settlements were largely confined to the several 'islands' of Ely, Ramsey and Thorney, which rose out of the low-lying landscape sufficiently to allow habitation all year round. The fens themselves were a rich habitat, with an abundance of freshwater fish and the possibility of crop cultivation in certain areas in summer. During the Middle Ages there were various localised attempts at draining fenland, but it was in the seventeenth century, in the decades either side of the Civil War, that 'adventurers', principal among them the Duke of Bedford, engaged the Dutch engineer Cornelius Vermuden to apply the techniques of land drainage developed so successfully in his home country. Vermuden employed large artificial rivers cut straight through the fen landscape to speed the flow of water from its inland sources to the sea and so successful did they prove to be that the water levels were greatly lowered. However, as soon as the land began to dry out its level dropped, creating the singular spectacle of rivers running above the level of the surrounding land. At first wind pumps were used to keep the lower levels dry and raising the water up the embankments and into the rivers and the drains which connected them; in the Victorian age these were replaced by steam pumps which in turn have been superseded by electric ones.

As the fenland became cultivable all year round, the rich soil made possible the growth of abundant crops. However, until the coming of the railways it was all but impossible to transport perishable goods like fruit and vegetables much beyond their source. Railways changed this, offering rapid transit to distant locations all over the country and thereby encouraging the growth of the towns and cities which were the products of the Industrial Revolution. The machine age of the nineteenth century produced ever more sophisticated machinery for use in agriculture, allowing for the more intensive cultivation of food, and the railways carried the coal which provided the steam to power them.

Railway building in the fens was relatively straightforward, the lie of the land offering few major obstacles requiring tunnelling or steep gradients. The techniques of constructing lines across wet or marshy terrain had been developed by George Stephenson on the Liverpool & Manchester Railway where it crossed Chat Moss and these were applied in the fens. The various drains needed bridging, sometimes with structures capable of opening to allow the passage of boats and barges, but possibly the most common feature of lines in the fens was the proliferation of level crossings, all needing staff to ensure the safe passage of trains. In addition to lines constructed and operated by the main-line railway companies there existed numerous industrial branches, often referred to as 'farmers' lines', which ran out into the fenland for the carriage of goods. These are beyond the scope of this book, which deals with passenger-carrying lines, but they are a fascinating aspect of the area.

After 1862 the Great Eastern Railway held an almost complete monopoly throughout East Anglia. The company's largest constituent was the Eastern Counties Railway, part of the empire of the 'Railway King', the famous – or infamous – George Hudson. His fall from grace due to dubious financial practices after the collapse of the 'Railway Mania' in the late 1840s left the Eastern Counties to contend with a new rival for the route from London to York, the Great Northern Railway, promoted by the coal owners of South Yorkshire and running to the west of the fens. The Eastern Counties had for a long time an unenviable reputation for delay and poor service but the Great Eastern strove to put this legacy behind it and became, by the end of the century, a progressive and well-managed company with extensive seafaring interests as well as its railway business.

Although Cambridgeshire was firmly within the Great Eastern orbit, the company did not have the county to itself. This was even more the case in Huntingdonshire, where the Great Northern's main line from London ran up the western side, making for Peterborough, which it developed into a large traffic centre. Through Huntingdonshire and Bedfordshire ran other lines, following an east-west orientation; principal among these were the London & North Western from Bletchley and Northampton, and the Midland, also from Northampton but also from Birmingham and Leicester, making for the Eastern Counties. Along the southern edges of the Wash, a miscellaneous collection of local lines were formed into a joint line, operated by the Midland and the Great Northern and eventually wending its way across Norfolk to Yarmouth.

As in so many other counties, rationalisation of the railway network has tended to see the survival of the older routes, particularly those radiating out from London, while the more recent additions to the network have succumbed to closure. Even so, both counties covered by this book have seen not only the survival of main routes, but their development, including electrification. It remains possible to travel from Peterborough to London both through Huntingdon and Cambridge; it is pleasant to think that George Hudson might have approved.

Cambridge – Bedford *

Passenger service withdrawn	1 January 1968	*Station closed*	*Date of closure*
Distance	29¾ miles	Old North Road	1 January 1968
Original owning company	Bedford & Cambridge Railway	Gamlingay	1 January 1968

Station closed	*Date of closure*
Lord's Bridge	1 January 1968

* The closed stations on this line that were in Bedforshire were Potton, Sandy, Blunham and Willington.

A London North Western Railway 0-6-0 entering Lord's Bridge Station with a train including a horsebox and two carriages.

Cambridge was one of the principal stations on the Great Eastern system, but, as noted in the Introduction, also played host to other companies' trains. One of these was the London & North Western Railway, which operated a long, straggling line from Oxford Rewley Road, hard by the Great Western station, to Cambridge, via Bletchley and Bedford. The most easterly section was originally incorporated as the Bedford & Cambridge Railway under an Act of 1860, work beginning the following year. The company acquired the Sandy & Potton Railway and incorporated it into its route, resulting in the sale of one of its engines, named Shannon, which eventually became the property of the Wantage Tramway in Oxfordshire and is now in the keeping of the Great Western Society at Didcot.

Old North Road Station, c. 1905.

The line opened from 1 August 1862, but its financial position was precarious and it was incorporated into the LNWR from 23 June 1864. This gave that company a 76½-mile route between the two university towns, over which trains made leisurely journeys, taking between two-and-a-half to three hours in 1910, calling at all 22 intermediate stations and crossing the Anglo-Scottish main lines of the London & North Western, the Midland and the Great Northern in the process. In later years the LMS operated its experimental three-car diesel train over the line from 1938, but this ceased with the outbreak of war the following year.

Cross-country lines like this were easy targets for the economies of the late 1950s and 1960s and the line eventually closed between Bedford and Cambridge on the first day of 1968. A section near Old North Road was later converted for the use of a mobile radio telescope owned by the University of Cambridge.

Cambridge – Mildenhall *

Passenger service withdrawn	18 June 1962
Distance	20¾ miles
Original owning company	Great Eastern Railway

Station closed	Date of closure
Barnwell Junction	18 June 1962
Fen Ditton Halt †	18 June 1962
Quy	18 June 1962
Bottisham & Lode**	18 June 1962
Swaffham Prior	18 June 1962
Burwell	18 June 1962
Exning Road Halt †	18 June 1962
Fordham ***	13 September 1965
Isleham	18 June 1962
Worlington Golf Links Halt **** †	18 June 1962

*   The closed station on this line that was in Suffolk was Mildenhall.
**   Originally named Bottisham; '& Lode' added in 1897.
*** Originally named Fordham and Burwell until 2 June 1884. This remained open after the Mildenhall branch closed.
**** Originally named Mildenhall Golf Links Halt until 1 January 1923.
†   The halts were opened 20 November 1922.

Quy Station, June 1953.

Bottisham & Lode Station, June 1955.

The first section of the branch line to Mildenhall, between Cambridge and Fordham, on the line between Bury St Edmunds and Ely, opened on 2 June 1884 with the 7¼-mile section thence to Mildenhall on 1 April the following year. Mildenhall was a market town which for most of the line's existence was a small centre adjoining the fens. Change came with the Second World War when the United States Army Air Force established a large bomber station near the town, which added to the traffic, though in the end not enough to keep the line in existence.

Swaffham Prior Station, November 1961.

Traffic over the line always tended to be sparse and for most of the time during the early twentieth century a two-coach push-pull train, introduced in 1913, was more than adequate. In the line's later days it became a stronghold of the last of the Holden 'Intermediate' 2-4-0 tender engines (LNER class E4) on trains of ancient coaches, services usually running through to and from Cambridge, including British Railways No. 62785, now preserved under its former identity as Great Eastern No. 490 by the National Railway Museum. Indeed, Cambridge University Railway Society would hire an E4 and train for trips over the branch on Saturdays from time to time and students could even try their hand at driving the engine, a facility probably unique in the history of excursions. The E4's gave way to diesel railbuses in 1958, but these were insufficient to secure the line's future and it closed to passengers on 18 June 1962, goods services to Mildenhall ending two years later.

Fordham Station, c. 1910.

Isleham Station, *c.* 1910.

Great Chesterford – Newmarket *

Passenger service withdrawn	9 October 1851
Distance	16¾ miles
Original owning company	Newmarket & Chesterford Railway

Station closed	Date of closure
Bourne Bridge **	9 October 1851
Abington **	9 October 1851
Balsham Road **	9 October 1851

* Other original stations along the route are listed under the Cambridge – Newmarket line in the section Stations Closed on Lines Still Open to Passengers.

** Closed between 1 July and 9 September 1850.

This section of line was promoted during the latter part of the 1845-48 'Railway Mania', which witnessed a rash of speculation in railways, often of highly improbable lines whose promoters promised equally improbable returns on investments. Like all speculative 'bubbles' the Mania eventually collapsed under the weight of its own promises, but not soon enough to see both the promotion and construction of the Newmarket & Chesterford Railway, which opened on 3 January 1848 to goods and 4 April to passengers.

The N&CR was a project of George Hudson, the 'Railway King', who sought to create a line from London to Scotland joining up his railway interests in eastern England. The intention was to avoid Cambridge by striking off the Northern & Eastern Railway route at Great Chesterford and joining the Norfolk Railway at Thetford. This involved a shorter route than that of the Eastern Counties Railway, but money was becoming increasingly scarce as the Mania foundered and the company's creditors closed in, resulting in a three-month suspension of services from 30 June 1850. Eventually nemesis struck and from 9 October 1851 the greater part of the line closed, the section between Six Mile Bottom and Newmarket being incorporated into the through route from Cambridge to Bury St Edmunds. The track was lifted, the rolling stock and six locomotives being acquired by the Great Eastern, successor to the Eastern Counties.

Over the years there were several attempts to resurrect the line, generally from aristocratic supporters of the races at Newmarket, for whom the line would have avoided congestion at Cambridge. The most prestigious attempt, in 1892, was supported by the Duke of York (later George V), but the Great Eastern, who certainly had no intention of recreating a route which would duplicate others and be largely unused for much of the year, turned a respectful but very determined deaf ear. The route can still be traced in places, but this was one of the earliest examples of a steam passenger railway closure over a century before the infamous Beeching cuts.

Cambridge Station is still in service but has changed since this *c.* 1900 photograph.

Holme – Ramsey

Passenger service withdrawn   6 October 1947
Distance   5¾ miles
Original owning company   Ramsey Railway

Station closed	Date of closure
St Mary's	6 October 1947
Ramsey North *	6 October 1947

* Originally named Ramsey until 1 July 1923.

Holme Station.

St Mary's Station after closure to passengers, April 1957. Goods traffic continued into the early 1970s.

Ramsey's significance in the fenland region was reinforced by having two separate railways running to it. The first of these chronologically was the Ramsey Railway, promoted as an independent company by an Act of 1861 and opened on 22 July 1863. Four years later, in 1867, it was absorbed into the Great Eastern Railway, though its main line connection was to the Great Northern's main line at Holme. Curiously, in some respects, it was subsequently leased to, and operated by, the Great Northern from 1875. Possibly these arrangements were a reflection of the inordinate time taken to build the other line to Ramsey, described in a separate section.

As with the Great Eastern line from Somersham, the Holme – Ramsey line had a lean time for traffic, though Bradshaw reported seven trains each way on weekdays in 1910, three extras being provided on Saturdays. With the closure of the Great Eastern route in 1930 this became the only regular passenger service to the town, but it did not survive to see nationalisation, being withdrawn in October 1947. Goods traffic continued until 1973, leaving Ramsey without rail connections.

Kettering – Huntingdon – Cambridge

Passenger service withdrawn   11 September 1959
Distance   47¾ miles
Original owning company   Kettering, Thrapstone & Huntingdon Railway / Ely & Huntingdon Railway

Station closed	*Date of closure*
Kimbolton	15 June 1959
Grafham **	15 June 1959
Buckden ***	15 June 1959
St Ives	5 October 1970
Godmanchester ****	15 June 1959
Swavesey	5 October 1970
Long Stanton	5 October 1970
Oakington	5 October 1970
Histon	5 October 1970

* The closed stations on this line that were in Northamptonshire were Cranford, Twywell, Thrapston Midland Road and Raunds.
** Originally named Graffham until 1 February 1877.
*** Originally named Brampton until 1 February 1868.
**** Originally named Huntingdon until 1 July 1882.

Kimbolton Station, August 1958.

Grafham Station, c. 1910.

The Midland Railway's reputation as 'the Octopus', spreading tentacles in all directions, included a cross-country route eastwards from Kettering, on the company's main line to the Midlands from St Pancras, to Huntingdon and Cambridge. The idea of such a line went back to a plan by the South Midland Railway in 1846 during the 'Railway Mania', but it failed to materialise. In 1862 the scheme was revisited, this time by the Kettering, Thrapstone & Huntingdon Railway, which made an agreement with the Midland to work the line; running powers over the St Ives to Cambridge section were negotiated with the Great Eastern. Goods traffic commenced on 21 February 1866, passenger traffic following on 1 March. The KT&HR remained independent until absorbed by the Midland from 6 August 1897.

Buckden Station, c. 1910.

Like other cross-country routes, the area through which it passed was relatively thinly populated and traffic tended to be sparse as a result. In 1910 four trains plied the route daily in each direction, taking between one-and-a-half to two hours, calling at all stations between Kettering and St Ives. Unsurprisingly, the Midland, a company notably reluctant to dispose of ancient engines, tended to work the line with some of its more venerable motive power; this was a tradition continued by the LMS which employed the last Kirtley double-framed four-coupled tender engines on passenger trains, including the now preserved 158A. Attractive though this might be to enthusiasts, ordinary travellers were probably less enamoured of such leisurely progress. Stations at the western end were progressively closed during the 1950s and the entire route succumbed from 5 October 1970.

St Ives Station.

The ornate crossing keeper's cottage at Godmanchester Station, August 1953. The main station buildings are in the background on the left.

Swavesey Station looking to the level crossing with the station on the right.

Long Stanton Station.

Oakington Station, *c.* 1920.

Histon Station.

KETTERING – HUNTINGDON – CAMBRIDGE

March – Magdalen Road *

Passenger service withdrawn	9 September 1968
Distance	11¾ miles
Original owning company	East Anglian Railway

Station closed	Date of closure
Wisbeach East **	9 September 1968

* The closed stations on this line that were in Norfolk were Emneth, Smeeth Road, Middle Drove and Magdalen Road.
** Originally named Wisbeach; renamed Wisbech from 4 May 1877 until 27 September 1948.

Wisbech East Station, May 1953.

The East Anglian Railway was very much the poor relation of the Eastern Counties Railway, the latter originally being part of the network of companies created by the 'Railway King', George Hudson, during the 1840s as part of a grand scheme for a railway from London to York. In 1845 the EAR was responsible for promoting a line from Kings Lynn to Wisbech, which received its Act in June of that year. The line branched westward off the route from Kings Lynn to Cambridge at Magdalen Road, making its way to March by way of Wisbech. It offered a useful route from the north Norfolk line to Norwich and Peterborough, from where connections carried traffic to and from the towns and cities of the Midlands. The East Anglian Railway was incorporated into the Great Eastern Railway in August 1872.

By the early years of the twentieth century the passenger service was operated from Peterborough to Kings Lynn and consisted of eight trains in each direction on weekdays. The line survived the initial round of cuts under the Beeching reorganisation in the mid-1960s, though the goods service ended on 5 October 1964. Passenger services continued until 9 September 1968, the closure depriving Wisbech of its second route – the Midland & Great Northern Joint being the other – and making March its nearest railhead.

March – Spalding *

Passenger service withdrawn	11 September 1961	*Station closed*	*Date of closure*
Distance	19½ miles	Murrow West **	6 July 1953
Original owning company	Great Northern Railway		
	/ Great Northern & Great Eastern Joint Committee from 1882	* Closed stations on this line that were in Lincolnshire were French Grove & Gedney Hill, Cowbit and Portland.	
Station closed	*Date of closure*	** Originally named Murrow until 27 September 1948.	
Guyhirne	5 October 1953		

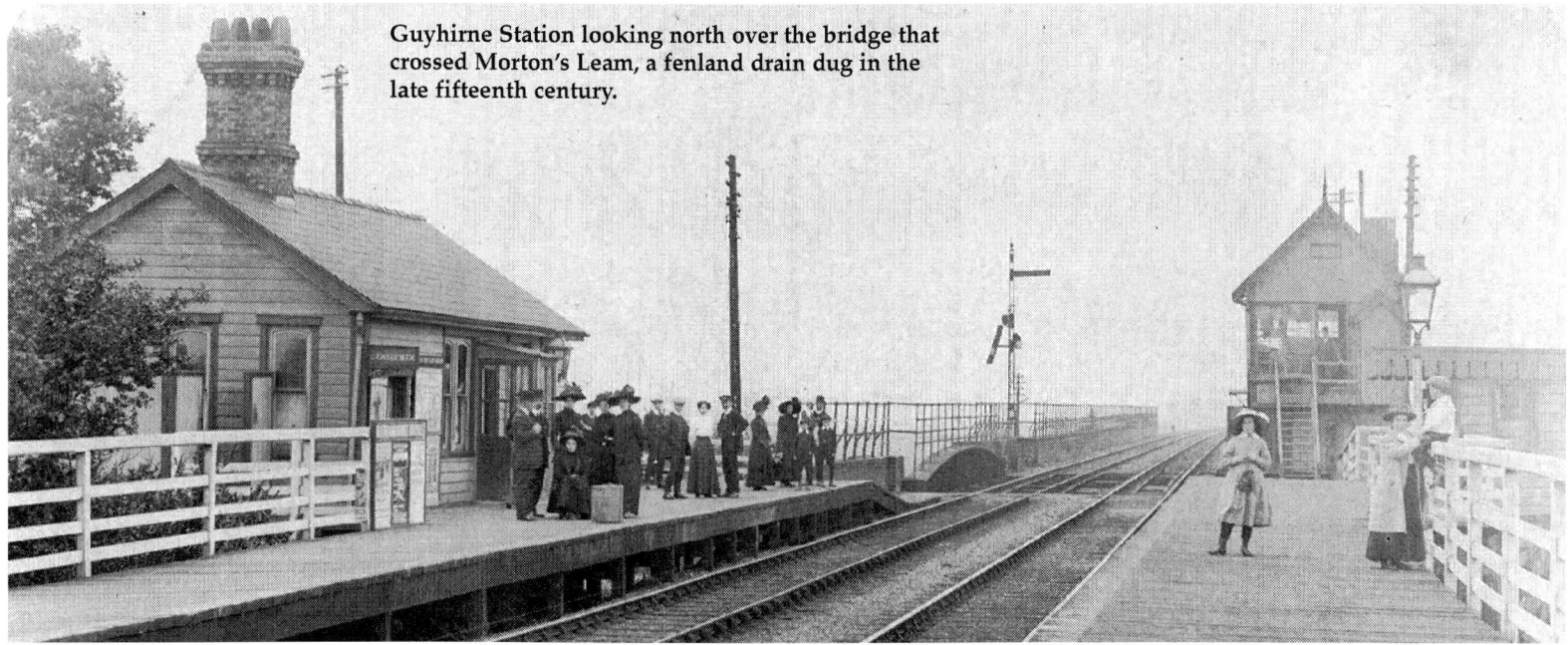

Guyhirne Station looking north over the bridge that crossed Morton's Leam, a fenland drain dug in the late fifteenth century.

The origins of the Great Northern & Great Eastern Joint line, much of which was originally built and owned solely by the Great Northern, lie in a succession of attempts by the Great Eastern Railway from its formation in 1862 to gain a route north out of East Anglia through Lincolnshire towards the coalfields of the east Midlands and south Yorkshire. Unsurprisingly, this alarmed the Great Northern, which tended to regard most of Lincolnshire in much the same way as the Great Eastern regarded East Anglia. Eventually a compromise was reached, saving the Great Eastern the cost of a ruinously expensive route duplicating the Great Northern as far north as Doncaster. A certain amount of new construction, primarily between Sleaford and Lincoln, with an avoiding line around the latter city, was needed and the Great Northern vested its route in the control of a joint committee of the two companies which continued in existence until the Grouping of 1923 rendered it unnecessary. From 1897 the Great Eastern also gained access to Nottinghamshire and

Murrow West Station looking from the flat crossing with the Midland & Great Northern Railway's line from Peterborough to Sutton Bridge.

Derbyshire off the joint line with the opening of the Lancashire, Derbyshire & East Coast Railway from Chesterfield to Lincoln, which continued after the LD&ECR was vested in the Great Central Railway a decade later.

The Joint Line, as it was often referred to, was a vital link for goods traffic between Yorkshire and East Anglia, having the great virtue of offering an alternative to sending large volumes of traffic down the Great Northern main line between Doncaster and Peterborough. The marshalling yard at Whitemoor, near March, was created in the 1920s to deal with the huge flows of traffic north and south; it was modernised in 1931 with what at the time was regarded as state-of-the-art equipment including a 'hump' layout and hydraulic retarders to guide the progress of wagons down into the fans of sidings leading from it. With the decline in goods traffic, Whitemoor contracted and eventually gradually closed in the 1990s, though a limited revival of facilities has followed in the early years of the twenty-first century. No such reprieve was granted to the Joint Line south of Spalding, which closed to passengers in 1961 and completely in 1970.

Peterborough – Seaton *

Passenger service withdrawn   4 May 1964
Distance   19½ miles
Original owning company   London & Birmingham / London & North Western Railway

Station closed	Date of closure
Peterborough East **	6 June 1966
Wansford ***	1 July 1957 [see text]

* The closed stations on this line that were in Northamptonshire were Orton Waterville, Castor, Nassington, Kingscliffe and Wakerley & Barrowden. The closed station in Rutland was Seaton.
** Originally named Peterborough until 1 July 1923.
*** Originally named Sibson until 1 January 1870.

Peterborough East Station, June 1931.

This line represents a further attempt by the London & North Western Railway to construct a route to East Anglia, in this case for traffic from Birmingham. The Rugby – Market Harborough line had opened in 1850, having been a project of that pioneering long-distance main line, the London & Birmingham Railway. During the 1870s, wishing for a more direct route from Birmingham, the LNWR constructed a line from Seaton eastwards along the Nene valley to Wansford and thereby gained access to Peterborough and the Great Eastern Railway. The line opened from 1 November 1879, thereby relegating the original route from Seaton to the Midland Railway at Luffenham to the status of a branch, off which a further branch struck off to Uppingham.

A crowd gathers by an unusual visitor to Wansford Station, a Michelin railcar. Inspired by the success of Michelin's pneumatic rubber wheeled railcars in France in the early 1930s Armstrong Siddley brought the concept to Britain. Partnering with the French company and the LMS they produced two vehicles for trials in 1935. The railcars were popular with passengers and crew but operational difficulties, such as the load limit of the tyres and the problem of flats meant that by 1937 the trials had ended and the railcars were placed in storage. They were dismantled after the Second World War and all that remains is a single wheel.

The new route was an important secondary main line in the pre-nationalisation period, carrying traffic for Harwich and Yarmouth. It also carried traffic for the Great Northern from Peterborough to Leicester in pre-Grouping days. After 1948, however, the former Midland route from Leicester to Peterborough was given priority and the LNWR route was relegated to a secondary cross-country line and it closed from 6 June 1966.

Although the greater part of the line is no longer in use, rebirth came for the six-and-a-half miles from Peterborough to Wansford when the Nene Valley Railway was created as a joint enterprise between the Peterborough Locomotive Society and Peterborough District Council, which was in process of establishing a 'linear park' along the line of the railway. The line's operational headquarters are at the restored Wansford station and the first train in public service ran on 1 June 1977. The line has played host to an interesting collection of European locomotives and rolling stock, though a good deal of British equipment also operates there.

Peterborough – Sutton Bridge *

Passenger service withdrawn   2 March 1959
Distance   28½ miles
Original owning company   Peterborough, Wisbeach and Sutton Railway

Station closed	Date of closure
Thorney	2 December 1957
Wryde	2 December 1957
Murrow **	2 March 1959
Wisbech St Mary ***	2 March 1959
Wisbech North ****	2 March 1959

* The closed station on this line that was in Norfolk was Ferry. The closed station in Northamptonshire was Eye Green for Crowland and those in Lincolnshire were Tydd and Sutton Bridge.
** Renamed Murrow East from 27 September 1948.
*** Originally named Wisbech St Mary [Midland] until 4 May 1877.
**** Originally named Wisbeach [Midland] until 4 May 1877; renamed Wisbech until 27 September 1948.

Wryde Station.

The story of the Midland & Great Northern Joint Railway has been told in several other volumes of this Lost Railways series, specifically those covering Lincolnshire, Norfolk and Suffolk – testimony in itself to the scale and scope of this network of lines which came into being in order to challenge the monopoly of the Great Eastern Railway throughout East Anglia and, in due course, to allow its rivals, the Great Northern and the Midland, to gain access to Norfolk and Suffolk.

Murrow Station. The flat junction on the March – Spalding line is out of sight in the distance.

The section of the network from Peterborough to Sutton Bridge was promoted as the Peterborough, Wisbeach and Sutton Railway, which received its parliamentary Act in July 1863. It opened to goods traffic on 1 June 1866 and to passengers exactly two months later. It was incorporated into the Eastern & Midland Railway from 1 July 1883 and thereby became part of the Midland & Great Northern Joint Railway from 1 July 1893. The company's Act had included clauses to allow it to make arrangements with both the Great Northern and the Midland, but it was the latter which acted first and undertook to work the line for 50% of gross receipts. In time this caused bad relations with the Eastern & Midland company, which complained that the Midland sent more goods over its line from Bourne to Kings Lynn than it routed through Wisbech.

The platform bridge of Wisbech Station decorated to welcome home Lord Peckover, 16 July 1907. Alexander Peckover was a Quaker banker who became Lord Lieutenant of Cambridgeshire. On retiring he was granted a peerage. He became Lord Peckover of Wisbech in King Edward VII's Birthday Honours, 28 June 1907. It was said he was both the first Quaker to be Lord Lieutenant and first to sit in the House of Lords.

The creation of the Joint Committee in 1893 enabled the system to be worked as a whole and from then until the Great War the M&GN enjoyed its period of greatest prosperity. After the Grouping the inclusion of both the Great Northern and Great Eastern in the London & North Eastern Railway tended to reduce the importance of the former penetrating the territory of the latter. As the inter-war years progressed the M&GN became increasingly reliant on large volumes of summer Saturday traffic to and from the east coast resorts; the considerable demands of working these over a primarily single-track route were handled with legendary efficiency. The imbalance between frantically busy holiday traffic, over a far shorter season than is the case today, impaired the viability of the system and during the 1950s it was decided that it could only continue to handle traffic if significant bridge renewals were not required. When they became necessary towards the end of the decade the decision was taken to close the entire system, which was done from 2 March 1959. At the time such an extensive closure was unprecedented, but the demise of the M&GN became a foretaste of the epidemic of closures which followed in the following decade.

St Ives – Ely

Passenger service withdrawn	2 February 1931	*Station closed*	*Date of closure*
Distance	17¾ miles	Sutton [first station]	10 May 1878
Original owning company	Ely, Haddenham & Sutton Railway	Sutton [second station] *	2 February 1931
		Haddenham	2 February 1931
Station closed	*Date of closure*	Wilburton	2 February 1931
Bluntisham	2 February 1931	Stretham	2 February 1931
Earith Bridge	2 February 1931		

* Reopened in 1948 as Sutton (E.R.) by British Rail and closed after 1956.

Bluntisham Station, *c.* 1930.

This was a fenland railway constructed by a local company and built without major earthworks. It was built in two sections: the first, from Ely to Sutton, was authorised by an Act of 23 June 1864, while the second section, from Sutton to St Ives, was authorised in 1876. Ely – Sutton opened on 16 April 1866 and trains began running to St Ives from 10 May 1878. The Ely, Haddenham & Sutton Railway was absorbed by the Great Eastern in 1898, though it had worked the line from its opening.

Earith Bridge Station.

The route was arranged to serve the greatest number of communities but stations were often at a distance from their namesakes. Bradshaw recorded a service of three trains a day each way Mondays to Saturdays, with an extra return trip on Mondays and Thursdays, but no Sunday service. Unsurprisingly the line was an early candidate for closure, passenger services ceasing from 2 February 1931, though excursions – mainly for the east coast – continued to use the line until 1957. Goods traffic ended between Bluntisham and Sutton in October 1958 and the line closed completely from 5 October 1964.

Sutton Station.

THE STATION SUTTON, CAMBS.

Wilburton Station.

St Ives – March

Passenger service withdrawn	6 March 1967
Distance	19 miles
Original owning company	Wisbech, St Ives & Cambridge Junction Railway

Station closed	Date of closure
Somersham	6 March 1967
Chatteris	6 March 1967
Wimblington	6 March 1967

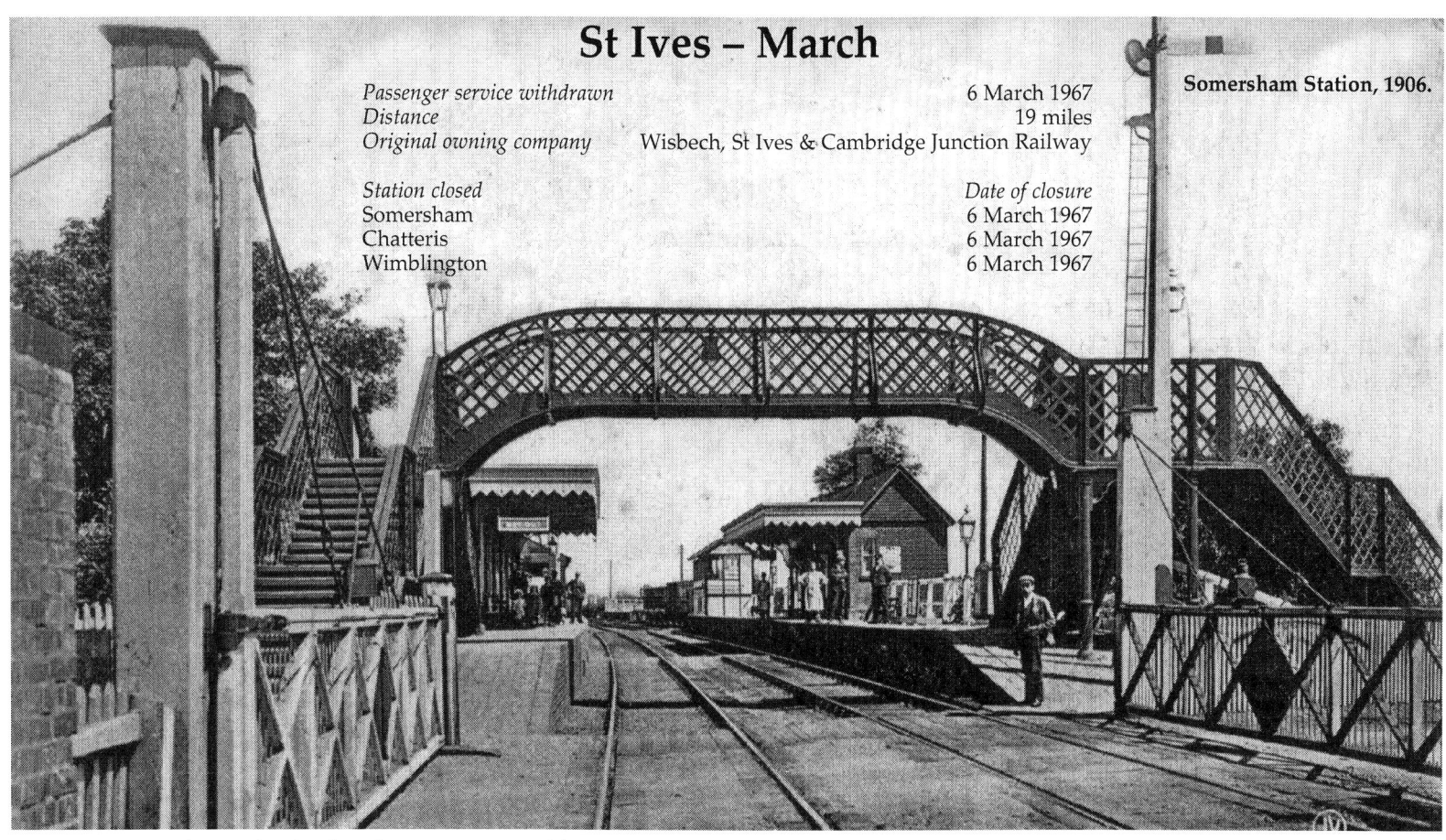

Somersham Station, 1906.

This route across the Cambridgeshire fens was promoted by the Wisbech, St Ives & Cambridge Junction Railway's Act of 1846 and constructed quickly, opening from 1 February 1848; the speed of construction reflected the easy terrain it covered. In 1847 it had been incorporated in the Eastern Counties Railway, becoming part of the Great Eastern Railway on its formation in 1862. From 1882 it was vested in the Great Northern & Great Eastern Joint Committee as part of the Great Eastern contribution to that enterprise.

Like the GN&GE line further north, this section carried a relatively modest passenger traffic – seven trains each way on weekdays in 1910 – but a considerable volume of goods, not least the long coal trains from pits in the east Midlands and south Yorkshire heading through the eastern counties and towards London. As further north, the decline of this traffic in the post-1945 era led to gradual closure, the spur to Chatteris Dock going in December 1955, the remaining goods facilities in April 1966 and finally the passenger service from 6 March 1967.

Somersham – Ramsey

Passenger service withdrawn	22 September 1930	Station closed	Date of closure
Distance	7 miles	Warboys	22 September 1930
Original owning company	Ramsey & Somersham Railway	Ramsey East *	22 September 1930

Station closed	Date of closure	
Somersham	6 March 1967	* Originally named Ramsey High Street until 1 July 1923.

Somersham Station where the last ever train for Ramsey is about to depart, Saturday 20 September 1930.

Warboys Station, August 1952.

Ramsey is one of the historic 'islands' of the fens, along with Ely and Thorney, areas of raised ground originally rising out of the marsh and meres and latterly, after the fen drainage schemes from the seventeenth century onwards, becoming centres of population and trade. The Ramsey & Somersham Railway, incorporated by its Act of 2 June 1865, projected a line from the then Great Eastern St Ives – March line to Ramsey. Construction was a long, drawn-out process, the seven miles eventually opening on 16 September 1889. From 1 January 1897 it was incorporated into the Great Northern & Great Eastern Joint Committee.

The line skirted around Ramsey and there was a hope that it would make an end-on connection with the branch from Holme to Ramsey, though this never materialised. Traffic was sparse, though seven passenger trains a day plied the route in each direction in 1910, Bradshaw including in the timetable connections to and from London. The passenger service ended on 22 September 1930, though occasional excursion traffic continued for some years afterwards. Goods traffic from Warboys to Ramsey lingered on until September 1956 and the line finally closed completely from 13 July 1964.

Wisbech – Upwell *

Passenger service withdrawn	2 January 1928
Distance	7¾ miles
Original owning company	Great Eastern Railway

Station closed	*Date of closure*
Outwell Village **	2 January 1928

*   The closed stations on this line that were in Norfolk were Elm Bridge, Boyce's Bridge, Outwell Basin and Upwell.
** Officially closed to passengers from Monday 2 January 1928, though the last trains ran on Saturday 31 December 1927.

Elm Road in Wisbech. Behind the train the track curves to the left and Wisbech Station.

The Wisbech & Upwell was an example of a rural roadside tramway, something common in many parts of Europe, with several in Ireland, but most unusual in Scotland, Wales and England. Indeed the Wisbech & Upwell was the first such tramway in Britain.

Outwell village where a tram is in the depot and about to cross the road that leads to St Clement's church.

The need to transport fruit and vegetables quickly from the rich farming country south of the ancient port of Wisbech to markets across Britain led local promoters to consider a railway out into the fens from the mid-1860s. In 1873 the Upwell, Outwell & Wisbech Railway obtained an Act for the construction of a line of a little over 6¼ miles to connect with the Great Eastern Railway at Wisbech. The promoters attempted to interest the Great Eastern in arrangements to work the line on their behalf, but the company showed little interest. The five years allowed by the Act for the construction of the line were almost expired when in 1880 the Great Eastern suddenly showed interest in the idea. However, they chose to promote their own line of a largely similar route and, since no work had been done in building the independent line, its powers lapsed. The Great Eastern's Act authorising the tramway was passed in July 1881. The first trains ran, as far as Outwell Basin, on 20 August 1883 and the service was extended to Upwell from 8 September 1884.

The line was built to follow existing public roads for much of its length and detailed arrangements were made to ensure the safety of pedestrians and other road users, especially those using horses. The carriages were of the 'tramcar' type with open saloons rather than compartments, which were entered from verandahs at each end; goods were carried in ordinary wagons and vans, since these needed to be handed over to the main lines for transit to their destinations. Locomotives were of a wholly different appearance to conventional designs, having side sheets covering their wheels and motion and animal fenders at either end. The boiler was enclosed within a wooden body, making them resemble a goods brake van, and controls were arranged to allow the engines to be driven from either end. Governors were fitted which restricted the maximum speed to 8 mph, later raised to 12 mph.

The crossing in Outwell village looking towards the tram depot.

The tramway was successful as a carrier of goods, particularly perishables, and was initially successful in carrying passengers, most of whom were content to live with the inevitable delays caused by the mixed trains shunting goods traffic at intermediate stops. Although there were designated stopping places, trains would stop to pick up and set down passengers at any convenient point along the line. However, in the years after the Great War the development of road transport presented a challenge to the passenger traffic which the tramway was unable to resist and the London & North Eastern Railway, as successors to the Great Eastern, withdrew the passenger service at the end of 1927.

The goods traffic along the line was less immediately affected by road transport, since lorries were not practicable as long-distance carriers; though as the years went by this situation changed significantly. The second world war gave the line a respite, but as road hauliers became more adept at cornering long-distance traffic the tramway's fate was sealed. The last train ran on Friday 20 May 1966.

The route of the line can still be traced in many places, often in the form of a broad roadside verge. The line gained a good deal of attention from enthusiasts over the years and even achieved a place in children's literature. The Rector of Emneth in the early 1950s was the Rev. Wilbert Awdry, who immortalised the steam locomotives on the tramway through the character Toby the Tram Engine in his famous tales about Thomas the Tank Engine. The outline of the steam engines has become a local motif, seen on the roadside signs of the communities along the route which the tramway once served. If the tram has long gone, it certainly has not been forgotten.

Stations closed on lines still open to passengers: Cambridge – Newmarket *

Original owning company Eastern Counties Railway

Stations closed *Date of closure*
Fulbourne 2 January 1967
Six Mile Bottom ** 2 January 1967

*   The closed station on this line that was in Suffolk was Newmarket [first station].
** Originally named Westley until October 1848.

Fulbourne Station *c.* 1910.

Six Mile Bottom Station.

Ely – March – Peterborough

Original owning company — Great Eastern Railway

Stations closed
Chettisham
Black Bank *
Stonea

Date of closure
13 June 1960
17 June 1963
7 November 1966

Stations closed
Peterborough East **

Date of closure
6 June 1966

* Originally named Little Downham until November 1853.
** Originally named Peterborough [GE] until 1 July 1923.

Chettisham Station.

Ely – Newmarket

Original owning company   Ely & Newmarket Railway

Stations closed	*Date of closure*
Soham *	13 September 1965
Fordham **	13 September 1965

*   A new station was opened at Soham on 13 December 2021.
**   Originally named Fordham & Burwell until 2 June 1884.

Soham Station, *c.* 1910.

Hitchin – Cambridge

Original owning company   Great Northern Railway (Hitchin – Shepreth)
/ Eastern Counties Railway (Shepreth – Cambridge)

Stations closed   *Date of closure*
Harston   17 June 1963

Hitchin – Peterborough [East Coast main line] *

Original owning company   Great Northern Railway

Stations closed   *Date of closure*
Three Counties **   5 January 1959
Offord & Buckden ***   2 February 1959
Abbots Ripton ****   15 September 1958
Holme   6 April 1959
Yaxley & Farcet *****   6 April 1959

*   The closed stations on this line that were in Bedfordshire were Tempsford and Arlesey & Henlow.
**   Originally named Arlesey Siding until 1 July 1886; reopened and renamed Arelesy on 3 October 1988. Its location was on the border of Cambridgeshire, Bedfordshire and Hertfordshire.
***   Originally named Offord until 1 August 1876.
****   Originally named Abbotts Ripton until 1938.
*****   Originally named Yaxley until July 1895.

Three Counties Station.

Abbots Ripton level crossing, *c.* 1910, about half a mile south of the station.

Abbots Ripton Station; the signal box has an extra 't' in Abbotts Ripton.

Yaxley & Farcet Station.